September Reed's
MANDALA
COLORING BOOK

September Reed's
MANDALA
COLORING BOOK

SIRIUS

About September Reed

September Reed was born with a passion for color and creative expression. While she explored apparel design and music professionally, her career turned a new corner when one day, out of curiosity and admiration for the art form, she began learning about henna body art (or Mehndi art). As she honed her drawing skills within this fascinating medium, she found herself especially drawn to mandala designs. Inspired by other Mehndi artists, she began using the same cones that she used for applying henna to skin to apply paint to canvas.

Custom requests for mandala paintings led to an exponential growth and development in September's art. Her favorite part of painting and drawing mandalas became the texture and delightful details that emerge from her paint cones. She uses acrylic paints of varying viscosity and finishes to bring luminescent light into her originals.

To connect with her audience, September started creating coloring pages and books based on her mandala paintings. This allowed her to share her passion while also encouraging her supporters to spend time exploring creativity for themselves. She currently works in various mediums and creates a variety of 3D art, which ranges from painted teapots to gilded headdresses.

The relationship between artist and audience is one that September considers crucial for her development, and the more she has been allowed to entertain and indulge in the whimsy of her clients, the more she's found fulfilment in sharing the joy that creating art has brought to her.

SIRIUS

This edition published in 2022 by Sirius Publishing, a division of Arcturus Publishing Limited,
26/27 Bickels Yard, 151–153 Bermondsey Street,
London SE1 3HA

ISBN: 978-1-3988-2573-4
CH010282NT
Supplier 29, Date 1022, PI 00002844

Printed in China

Introduction

Mandalas are an intricate form that can vary in infinite ways, and are found in many different cultures. Originating from the Sanskrit word meaning circles, mandalas have a history within Hindu beliefs as well as a notion that they represent a universe or realm within their borders. They are also often used as a focal point in meditation. They can be symbolic and spiritual, as well as contemporary and calming.

There is always a wonderful sense of serenity in my studio when I'm working on each of my designs, and the practice of creating mandalas is deeply soothing. While I learned many traditional elements and motifs during my Mehndi artist training, my designs are more often based around nature and flowing, floral elements, sometimes including characters or creatures as well. Each painting or drawing allows for a calm moment of Zen for myself, as well as for those who watch me paint my mandalas.

While I mostly paint my mandalas with acrylic on canvas, I've enjoyed expanding my designs into digital and printed form. I delight in the way that sharing coloring pages offers an opportunity for collaboration between myself and my audience. I believe we are all creative beings, but many are rarely encouraged toward art, nor are they given many opportunities to indulge their creative whims.

Process videos of my paintings can be found on my YouTube channel, Whimmmsy. More of my work and links can be found on my website *www.whimmmsy.com* and under the name *@whimmmsy* on social media.

September Reed

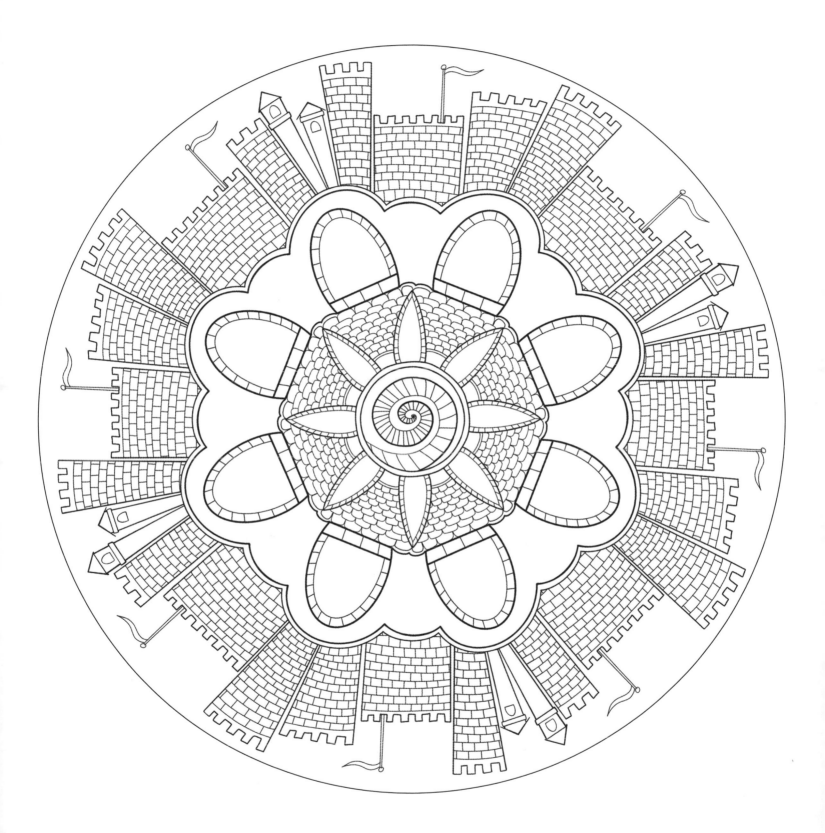